YOUNG PROFILES

Hilary Duff

Jill C. Wheeler

ABDO Publishing Company

visit us at
www.abdopub.com

Published by ABDO Publishing Company, 4940 Viking Drive, Edina, Minnesota 55435.
Copyright © 2004 by Abdo Consulting Group, Inc. International copyrights reserved in
all countries. No part of this book may be reproduced in any form without written
permission from the publisher.

Printed in the United States.

Cover Photo: Corbis
Interior Photos: AP/Wide World pp. 8, 24; Corbis p. 5; Getty Images pp. 7, 9, 11, 13, 15,
    16, 17, 19, 20, 21, 23, 25, 27, 29, 31

Editors: Kate A. Conley, Stephanie Hedlund, Kristianne E. Vieregger
Art Direction: Neil Klinepier

Library of Congress Cataloging-in-Publication Data

Wheeler, Jill C., 1964-
    Hilary Duff / Jill C. Wheeler.
        p. cm. -- (Young profiles)
    Includes index.
    Summary: Profiles the young actress known for her roles in the popular Disney
television series, "Lizzie McGuire," and in the movie, "Agent Cody Banks."
    ISBN 1-59197-407-0
    1. Duff, Hilary, 1987---Juvenile literature. 2. Actors--United States--Biography--
Juvenile literature. [1. Duff, Hilary, 1987- 2. Actors and actresses. 3. Women--
Biography.] I. Title. II. Series.

PN2287.D79W48 2003
792'.028'092--dc21
    [B]   2003042581

Contents

Teenage Sensation 4

Profile of Hilary Duff 6

Getting Started 8

On Television 10

Lizzie McGuire 12

In Love with *Lizzie* 14

Cadet Kelly 16

School on the Set 18

Singing Star 20

More Movies 22

Life of a Star 24

What Lies Ahead 28

Glossary 30

Web Sites 31

Index 32

Teenage Sensation

The 2002 holiday season was busy for Hilary Duff. She flew from Italy, where she was filming a movie, to Canada for more filming. Next, it was on to California to shoot a music video. Then, she flew to Florida before spending Christmas with her family in Texas.

While in Florida, Hilary taped a Christmas special. It was the 19th Annual Walt Disney World Christmas Day Parade. The parade aired on December 25, 2002.

Hilary was one of many Disney stars to appear in the holiday **gala**. However, she was the only one who could claim the lead in Disney's most popular television show. She could also claim a spot as one of Disney's newest singing stars. To top it off, she was only 15.

Hilary Duff

Profile of Hilary Duff

Name: Hilary Ann Duff

Date of Birth: September 28, 1987

Place of Birth: Houston, Texas

Current Home: Los Angeles, California

Height: Five feet, four inches

Parents: Bob and Susan Duff

Siblings: Older sister Haylie

Pets: Lil' Dog and Remington (dogs)

Job: Actress/singer

Hobbies: Singing, dancing, shopping

Favorite Stores: Bebe, Rampage, Wet Seal

Favorite Musicians: No Doubt, Nelly, Blink 182

Quote from Hilary: "If you really want something, don't give up. Don't quit, but be willing to work really hard, too."

Getting Started

Hilary Ann Duff was born on September 28, 1987, in Houston, Texas. Her father, Bob, is a partner in a convenience store chain. Her mother, Susan, works at home caring for Hilary and her older sister, Haylie.

Hilary began performing at age six. She was a dancer with the Columbus Ballet Met touring company. She danced in its performance of *The Nutcracker*. Hilary and her sister also took acting classes. Both girls quickly decided acting was the life for them.

Hilary on the set of
Lizzie McGuire

Hilary and Haylie learned an acting career was hard work. And, launching an acting career in Houston was even harder. Eventually, they convinced their mother to take them to Los Angeles, California. Their father stayed in Houston to run his business.

In Los Angeles, Hilary and her mom spent years meeting people and making contacts. Hilary went on many **auditions**. She got parts in a few commercials. Finally, she landed some small roles on television shows.

Hilary with her sister, Haylie

9

On Television

Hilary's first television job was in a miniseries called *True Women* in 1997. The next year, she played the young witch Wendy in the movie *Casper Meets Wendy*. She landed her first starring role in the television movie *The Soul Collector* in 1999. Hilary won a Young Artist Award for Best Supporting Actress for that role.

In 2000, Hilary had a role in an **episode** of the television show *Chicago Hope*. She worked with actor Tim Robbins in the film *Human Nature*. She also acted on stage with Sean Connery and Dennis Quaid in *Playing by Heart*. Meanwhile, her sister also found roles in television and movies.

Hilary credits her mother with much of the success she and Haylie have enjoyed. "My mom worked so hard for us," Hilary said. "It really wasn't easy, but we were pretty lucky."

In 2000, Hilary got what seemed to be her big break. The NBC television network was casting a new comedy called *Daddio*. Hilary was cast as one of the children on the show. After filming several **episodes**, Hilary learned that NBC had dropped *Daddio* from its lineup. She was crushed.

Hilary's bright and cheerful personality helps her win many roles.

Lizzie McGuire

After the disappointment with *Daddio*, Hilary wanted to leave show business altogether. Her mother talked her out of it. The following week, she learned she had won the lead role in a new Disney Channel show called *Lizzie McGuire*.

Hilary was surprised to hear she had landed the lead in *Lizzie*. She recalls the **audition** as very embarrassing. "The casting director was like, 'You are totally unprepared. Do you know any acting coaches?'" said Hilary. ". . . I wanted to get under a rock and hide."

Hilary's real-life personality made her perfect for the role, however. "*Lizzie McGuire* is about a fourteen-year-old girl from Anywhere, USA, just trying to find her way through life," Hilary said. "She has dorky parents she's embarrassed by. She has an annoying little brother and two good friends who are kind of dorky. There's also animated Lizzie, her **alter ego**, who is more sassy than regular Lizzie, who says things when Lizzie can't say it."

Hilary with some of her Lizzie McGuire *costars*

In Love with Lizzie

Disney made 65 **episodes** of *Lizzie McGuire*. They began airing in January 2001. They covered a range of normal teenage experiences. Lizzie has had to face everything from buying her first bra to getting her first kiss.

Lizzie McGuire rapidly became a hit. It ranked as one of the highest-rated **tween** series in the history of the network. It was also voted Favorite Television Series at Nickelodeon's 15th Annual Kids' Choice Awards in April 2002.

Lizzie became so popular Disney introduced a line of *Lizzie McGuire* clothing and accessories. "The clothes are pretty much what Lizzie wears," Hilary said. "Lots of glitter, rhinestones and cool pants." Hilary works with the costume designer to pick out what her character will wear on the show. She gets to keep the clothes at the end of the season.

Disney stopped shooting more **episodes** of the show in late 2002. That is common with shows about children. Hilary was growing up faster than her character. Disney sped up production on *Lizzie* to finish all 65 episodes before Hilary appeared too grown-up.

Hilary proudly smiles at the 2002 Kids' Choice Awards.

Cadet Kelly

It wasn't long before Disney **executives** realized they had a young star on their hands. So, they began making additional plans for Hilary. One of them was a movie made just for the Disney Channel.

Cadet Kelly is about a popular young girl named Kelly Collins. Kelly's mother marries a man in charge of a military school. Kelly has to move with her mom from New York City and attend the school. She hates it at first.

Hilary has a fashion style that is uniquely her own.

But gradually, she works at making the school more stylish and fun.

Hilary also had to work hard before they began filming the movie. "I trained for a whole month," she said. "We did lots of stunts in the movie, and I did the rifle training, tossing, and spinning."

Cadet Kelly aired in spring 2002. It became the Disney Channel's highest-rated original movie. It also earned honors as cable television's highest-rated movie to date in 2002.

Hilary Duff

School on the Set

A special challenge for young stars is keeping up in school. Filming a television series leaves little time for classes. Hilary usually arrived on the set of *Lizzie McGuire* at about seven in the morning. Often, she did not finish until just before five in the evening.

Despite the long hours on the set, California law requires young actors to have at least three hours of school each day. So, Hilary has a **tutor** on the set of her shows and movies. Hilary and her tutor squeeze in classes between shooting.

The three hours Hilary and her tutor spend together are hard work. "We go right to it," said Marsha Whittaker. Whittaker taught Hilary on the set of *Lizzie*. "There's no bell, traveling to class, or getting out our books."

When not working, Hilary is homeschooled. "My life is a lot different because I don't go to middle school," Hilary admitted. "I don't really go through some of the problems Lizzie goes through."

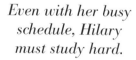

Even with her busy schedule, Hilary must study hard.

Singing Star

Hilary added a new job to her **résumé** in August 2002. She became a singer. Disney produced a **soundtrack** CD for *Lizzie McGuire*. Hilary sang the song "I Can't Wait" for the soundtrack.

"I Can't Wait" spent seven weeks at the number one spot on Radio Disney. Hilary made a music video of the song. It aired on the Disney Channel.

Hilary Duff

Hilary also worked on a Christmas CD called *Santa Claus Lane*. It hit stores in November 2002. The CD featured Hilary singing **solos** and **duets**. She sang the duet "Tell Me a Story" with **hip-hop** artist Lil' Romeo. Another song on the CD featured Hilary's sister, Haylie.

Hilary's singing career quickly took off after recording *Santa Claus Lane*. One of the songs from that CD landed on another **soundtrack**.

Hilary and her sister, Haylie, on the set of the game show Hollywood Squares

The *Santa Clause 2* soundtrack features Hilary singing the title track, "Santa Claus Lane." Hilary also contributed her version of "The Tiki Tiki Room" to Disney's new Disneymania CD. And, Hilary plans to release a new **solo** CD in fall 2003.

More Movies

Lizzie McGuire was a huge success for Disney. It was no surprise, then, when Disney **executives** decided to make a *Lizzie McGuire* movie. In the movie, Lizzie graduates from junior high. Then she goes on a trip to Rome, where she is mistaken for an Italian rock star. While working on the movie, Hilary traveled to Italy and Canada for filming.

Hilary has another movie in the works, too. In *Agent Cody Banks*, Hilary stars with Frankie Muniz. Muniz plays a young secret agent. Hilary plays Natalie Connors, a girl the secret agent must become friends with.

Hilary is also working on a remake of the 1950s movie, *Cheaper by the Dozen*. Then she will appear in a modern-day adaptation of *Cinderella*. The movie will be set in California. It is about a high-school student who is transformed into one of the prettiest girls in school.

Hilary with costar Frankie Muniz at the 2002 Kids' Choice Awards

Life of a Star

*L*izzie's success meant that suddenly almost everyone knew Hilary. At least, almost everyone under the age of 14 seemed to. "It was weird at first being recognized and stared at when at the mall or restaurants," Hilary said. "It's kind of embarrassing to go to the movies with friends and someone there goes, 'Oh, my God, it's Lizzie McGuire.' But it's nice to know that people like the show."

Hilary has learned to enjoy the extra attention she receives from her fans.

Hilary also had to deal with the lack of privacy so many stars face. For a while, Hilary dated young singer Aaron Carter. He guest starred on an **episode** of *Lizzie*. It seemed as though everyone knew about their relationship. "It was weird having a relationship with someone whom everybody knew . . . " Hilary said.

Hilary receives thousands of letters and emails from fans.

At home, Hilary tries to lead a normal life. She does chores, including taking out the trash and making her bed. She also takes care of her two dogs. She divides her time between Los Angeles and Houston. Her father often comes to Los Angeles to visit, too.

Hilary enjoys in-line skating, swimming, yo-yo tricks, and walking on her hands. Her favorite hobbies are hanging out with friends and shopping. She still enjoys dancing, just as she did when she was younger. However, now Hilary also enjoys **hip-hop** and **funk** dancing.

Hilary is also active in volunteer work, including being an animal rights **advocate**. In 2001, she served on the Youth Advisory Committee of Kids With A Cause. Kids With A Cause is a nonprofit group of famous children. The children work to help other children who are less fortunate.

Opposite page: Some of the Lizzie McGuire *cast members volunteer by planting trees.*

What Lies Ahead

Hilary will not be making any more *Lizzie McGuire* **episodes**. However, she has plenty of other projects to keep her busy.

The *Lizzie McGuire* clothing line is going strong, as is a *Lizzie McGuire* doll. Disney has talked of a possible new television series for Hilary, too. That series would be aimed at an older **audience** since Hilary is getting older.

Hilary says she is still more comfortable acting than singing. In fact, one of her dreams is to star as an action hero. "There are so many heroes for boys like Batman and Superman," she said. "There needs to be something for girls."

Hilary's future holds many new and exciting possibilities. One thing is certain, however. Whatever Hilary decides to do, she is sure to be a success.

Hilary Duff

Glossary

advocate - someone who works for and supports a cause.

alter ego - another aspect of oneself.

audience - a group of people watching a performance.

audition - a short performance to test someone's ability.

duet - a song sung by two performers.

episode - one show in a series of shows.

executives - people who are in charge of making the decisions in different businesses.

funk - a style of music that incorporates elements of blues music.

gala - a celebration.

hip-hop - a style of dancing, art, music, and dress that originated in urban areas and became popular through break dancing, graffiti, and rap music.

résumé - a list of accomplishments.

solo - a song sung by one performer.

soundtrack - an album containing the music played in a movie, play, or television show.

tutor - a teacher who gives private lessons to students.

tween - a young person between the ages of nine and 14.

Web Sites

To learn more about Hilary Duff, visit ABDO Publishing Company on the World Wide Web at **www.abdopub.com**. Web sites about Hilary are featured on our Book Links page. These links are routinely monitored and updated to provide the most current information available.

Fans from all over the world are waiting to see what Hilary's next success will be.

Index

A

Agent Cody Banks 22
awards 10, 14

C

Cadet Kelly 16, 17
California 4, 9, 18, 22, 26
Canada 4, 22
Carter, Aaron 25
Casper Meets Wendy 10
Cheaper by the Dozen 22
Chicago Hope 10
Columbus Ballet Met 8
Connery, Sean 10

D

Daddio 11, 12
Disney 4, 12, 14, 15, 16, 17, 20, 21, 22, 28
Disneymania CD 21

F

family 4, 8, 9, 10, 12, 21, 26
Florida 4

H

Houston, Texas 8, 9, 26
Human Nature 10

I

"I Can't Wait" 20
Italy 4, 22

K

Kids With A Cause 26

L

Lil' Romeo 20
Lizzie McGuire (movie) 22
Lizzie McGuire (soundtrack) 20
Lizzie McGuire (television show) 4, 12, 14, 15, 18, 20, 22, 24, 25, 28
Los Angeles, California 9, 26

M

Muniz, Frankie 22

N

NBC 11
New York City, New York 16

Nickelodeon 14
Nutcracker, The 8

P

Playing by Heart 10

Q

Quaid, Dennis 10

R

Robbins, Tim 10
Rome, Italy 22

S

Santa Claus Lane 20, 21
"Santa Claus Lane" 21
Santa Clause 2 21
Soul Collector, The 10

T

"Tell Me a Story" 20
Texas 4, 8, 9, 26
"Tiki Tiki Room, The" 21
True Women 10

W

Whittaker, Marsha 18